Soul's Journey to .Ya [God the Creator Yahweh]

What Happens To The Soul When A Person Dies

David Gomadza

www.twofuture.world

PAPERBACK : ISBN: 9798323694051

DEDICATION

A better future.

CONTENTS

ACKNOWLEDGMENTS

Tomorrow's World Order

WHAT HAPPENS TO THE SOUL WHEN A PERSON DIES

Soul's Journey to .Ya [God Creator Yahweh]
When a soul dies it must leave the body using several commands that makes it possible to go to heaven this it does through several commands most of which are predefined meaning depends on other things already predefined inside
Now if we look at what this predefined parameters are
1 the right to die and choose where to go where choosing depends on your actions here on earth
Now what counts as your actions your actions are the things you do here on earth when you are alive either according to Ya [creator] or the .devil [evil gamma]
Now if we Ask what can be done then we can predefined what is needed then we can find out what is needed to go to heaven or hell depending on our selection.

PREDEFINED PARAMETERS FOR HEAVEN.

Now this is the selection we must use if we want to go to heaven
We picked the first 100 things that are critical for your soul to automatically go to heaven
1] don't go to hell as a command

2] ask why ask.why
3] choose hell as second option only never maybe
4] ask what if most of the time [whatif.ask.why]
5] check what is [whatis.check.now]
6] don't talk about the devil in good way
7] never ask when as if to say when should I die as if your life is boring Yahweh love people who are full of life in death
8] ask when can we meet as a date with Yahweh
9] ask what if as if challenging status quo
10] ask why then if not [whythenifnot.ask.now]
11] ask whether is an option [whether.ask.option.now]
12] ask what was [whatwas.ask]
13] what if and when if [ask.whatifwhenif.start]
14] what can be and what would be [whatcanbe.ask.start.now]
15] what is but [what.is.but]
16] what could be [what.could be]
17] what has been [what.has.been]
18] what was and what is now [whatwaswhatis.ask]
19] what can be [what can be]
20] what will be [whatwillbe.ask]
21] what if [whatif.ask]
22] ask when and why [whenwhy.ask]
23] if not now then when [ifnotnowthenwhen]
[Everyonebinary.2.all.abyss.start.ifnot.fuel.ya.start.now]
24] why Now and not when [whynownotwhen.start]
25] if not then choose hell as second option [ifnotthenhellsecondchoice.start]
[zigzagxforever.start]
26] if not then what [ifnotthenwhat.start.now.initiate]
27] what can be [whatcanbe.start]
28] what could be can be [whatcouldbecanbe]
29] what was and is now [whatwasandisnow.start]
[Shit.shitty- mouth sealed forever]
30] what could be is and was but might not be [

whatcouldbeisbutmightnotbe.start]
31] what if [whatif.ask.start.now.ask.again.again]
32] what could be don't ask but ask what if instead [whatcouldbedontaskbutaskwhatifinstead.start]
33] what was and can still be and why [whatwasandstillcouldbeandwhy.srart]
34] what is and will be forever [whatisandwillbeforever]
35] what is to be [whatistobe.start]
36] what is but is not now [whatisbutisnotnow]
37] what could be and why [whatcouldbeandwhy.ask]
38] what was and when [whatwasandwhen.start]
39] what to be must be [whattobemustbe.ask.when.start]
40] what can be [whatcanbe.ask.now.start]
41] what was and could still be [whatwasandcouldstillbe.start]
42] what could be [whatcouldbe.start]
43] if not then what [ifnotthenwhat.ask]
44] what is but is not and why [whatisnotbutcouldbe.start]
45] if not now when then [ifnotnowwhenthen.start]
46] what is but must not be [whatisbutmustnotbe.start]
47] what could be [whatcouldbe.start]
48] what was and could still be [whatwasandcouldstillbe.start]
49] what will be but not now [whatwillbebutnotnow.start]
50] what was and is not but can be [whatwasandisnotbutcanbe.start]
51] what is to be and when [whatistobeandwhen.start]
52] what can be [whatcanbe.start]
53] what is to be can be [whatistobecanbe]
54] what is to be [whatistobe.start]
55] what was but... [whatwasbut....ask]
56] what can be but is not [whatcanbebutisnot.start]
57] what was [whatwas.ask]
58] what would be but is not [whatwouldbebutisnot.start]
59] to be [Tobe.ask]
60] to be to [tobeto.ask]

61] what is but [whatisbut.ask]
62] what could be [whatcouldbe.ask]
63] what was but is not [whatwasbutisnot.start]
64] what was but might not be [whatwasbutmightnotbe.start]
65] what if [whatif.start.ask.again.again.start]
66] what could be [whatcouldbe.start]
67] what was [whatwas.start]
68] what would be and why [whatwouldbeandwhy.start]
69] what might be but then [whatmightbebutthen.start]
70 what is to be but when [whatistobebutwhen.start]
71] what can be and why [whatcanbebutwhy.start]
72] what would be and why [whatwouldbeandwhy.start]
73] what was but is not [whatwasbutisnot]
74] what would be but [whatwouldbebut.start]
75] what can be but when [whatcanbebutwhen.start]
76] what was and is [whatwasandis.ask]
77] what could be but is not [whatcouldbebutisnotgt.ask]
78] what would be but when [whatwouldbebutwhen.ask]
79] what was but when [whatwasbutwhen.start]
80] what would be [whatwouldbe.start]
81] what was and is still not [whatwasandisstillness.start]
82] what was but could still [whatwasbutcouldstill.ask]
83] what would be [whatwouldbe.start]
84] what is to be [whatistobe.start.again.again.start.now.start]
85] what could be but [whatcouldbebut.start]
86] what was but how [whatwasbuthow.start]
87] to be but [tobebut.now.start]
88] what is to be [whatistobe.start]
89 what if [whatif.ya.start]
90] what can be but [whatcanbebut.start]
91] if we can ask what would be the answer
[ifwecanaskwhatwillbetheanswer.start]
92] what can be but [whatcanbebut.start]
93] what can be done [whatcanbedone.start]

94] what is to be done [whatistobedone.start]
95] what is to be [whatistobe.start]
96] what can be [whatcanbe.start.now.ask.start]
97] what is but is not [whatisbutisnot.start]
98] what is to be [whatistobe.when.start.now.start]
99] what is to be [whatistobe.start]
100] what is to be but why [whatistobebutwhy.start]
Now if we Ask these questions at the end we get a verdict and the reason based on these questions
David if not Yahweh where would he go if to die today and why
Yahweh can't be tested and after all he who sends people in abyss shall live forever no matter what because every sent shall extend his life with all his parts

2PREDEFINED PARAMETERS FOR HELL

Now if we are to ask what will need doing then we are going to go to hell and ask the predefined parameters for hell and as you will see hell and heaven use the same stencil as above the only difference is that every line for hell begins with hell.start and ends with whatthehell.whenthen that means we simply add a hell.start and a whatthehell.whenthen at the end of every bracketed answer for example the first line becomes

1] what the hell start what if [hell.startwhatif.whatthehell.whenthen
2] If hell then don't go to heaven
3] If not hell then heaven is second choice
4] What if it's hell then what
5] what can be said of hell
6] what is to be said of hell
7] what if [whatif.hellstart.whatthehell.whenthen]
8] what can be said of hell and why [whatcanbesaidofhellandwhy.hellstart.whatthehell.whenthen
9] what could be and why [whatcouldbeandwhy.hellstart.whatthehell.whenthen]
10] what can be said of hell [whatcanbesaidofhell.hellstart.whatthehell.whenthen]
11] what is to be and how [whatistobe.hellstart.whatthehell.whenthen]
12] what can be done [whatcanbedone.hellstart.whatthehell.whenthen
13] what could be [whatcouldbe.hellstart.whatthehell.whenhell]
14] what could be [whatcouldbe.hellstart.whathehell.whenthen]
15] what was before [hell.start.whatwasbefore.whatthehell.whenthen]
16] what can be becomes [hell.start.whatcanbe.whatthehell.whenthen]
17] what was [hell.start.whatwas.whatthehell.whenthen]

18] what to be [hell.start.whattobe.whatthehell.whenthen]
19] what can be done [hell.start.whatcanbedone.whatthehell.whenthen]
20] what is to be [hellstart.whatistobe.whatthehell.whenthen]
21] what is to be [hellstart.whatistobe.whatthehell.whenthen]
22] what can be is to be [hellstart.whatcanbeistobe.whatthehell.whenthen]
23] what was [hellstart.whatwas.whatthehell.whenthen]
24] what will be [hellstart.whatwillbe.whatthehell.whenthen]
25] what would be if [hellstart.whatthehell.whenthen]
26] if hell then what [hellstart.ifhellthenwhat.whatthehell.whenthen]
27] what can be [hellstart.whatcabne.whatthehell.whenthen]
28] what is to be but [hellstart.whatistobebut.whatthehell.whenthen]
29] what is to [hellstart.whatistobe.whatthehell.whenthen]
30] what was can still be [hellstart.whatwascanstillbe.whatthehell.whenthen]
31] what can be [hellstart.whatcanbe.whatthehell.whenthen]
32] what is to be [hellstart.whatistobe.whatthehell.whenthen]
33] what was then but can still be [hellstart.whatwasthenbutcanstillbe.whatthehell.whatthen]
34] to be [hellstart.tobe.whatthehell.whenthen]
35] what was but can still be [hellstart whatwasbutcanstillbe.whathehell.whenthen]
36] what can be [hellstart.whatcanbe.whatthehell.whenthen,]
37] what was is to be [hellstart.whatwssistobe.whatthehell.whenhell]
38] if hell start then what [hellstart.ifhellstartthenwhat.whatthehell.whenthen]
39] is to be but [hellstart.istobebut.whatthehell.whenthen]
40] what is to be [hellstart.whatistobe.whatthehell.whenthen]
41] is to be but when [hellstart.istobebutwhen.whatthehell.whenthen]
42] what is to be [hellstart.whatistobe.whathethell.whenthen]
43] what is to be but why [hellstart.whatistobebutwhy.whatthehell.whentgen]
44] what can be is to be [hellstart.whatcanbeistobe.whatthehell.whenthen]
45] what can be said [hellstart.whatcanbesaid.whatthehell.whenthen]
46] what is to be [hellstart.whatistobe.whatthehell.whenthen]
47] what if [hellstart.whatif.whatthehell.whenthen]
48] what is to be [hellstart.whatistobe.whenthen]
49] what was [hellstart.whatwas.whatthehell.whenthen]

50] what has been [hellstart.whathasbeen.whatthehell.whenthen]
51] what was [hellstart.whatwas.whatthehell.whatthen]
52] what is to be but can't be [
hellstart.whatistobebutcantbe.whatthehell.whenthen]
53] what is but will never be [
hellstart.whatisbutwillnevrrbe.whatthehell.whenthen]
54] what can be done [hellstart.whatcanbedone.whatthehell.whenthen]
55] to be but if not then how [
hellstart.tobebutifnotthenhow.whatthehell.whenthen]
56] what is to be [hellstart.whatistobe.whatthehell.qhenthen]
57] what can be [hellstart.whatcanbe.whatthehell.whenthen]
58] what was but could still be [
hellstart.whatwasbutcoulfdstillbe.whatthehell.whenthen]
59] what is but might not happen as such [
hellstart.whatisbutmightnothappenassuch.whatthehell.whenthen]
60] what can be said [hellstart.whatcanbesaid.whatthehell.whenthen]
61] what is to be [hellstart.whatistobe.whatthehell.whatthen]
62] what can be but might not be [
hellstart.whatcanbebutmightnotbe.whatthehell.whatthen]
63] what is to be [hellstart.whatistobe.whatthehell.whatthen]
64] what was [hellstart.whatwas.whatthehell.whenthen]
65] what is to be [hellstart.whatistobe.whatthehell.whatthen]
66] what can be [hellstart.whatcanbe.whatthehell.whenthen]
67] what is to be [hellstart.whatistobe.whatthehell.whatthen]
68] what can be [hellstart.whatcanbe.whatthehell.whatthen]
69] what can be said about this and why [
hellstart.whatcanbesaid.whatthehell.whenthen]
70] what is to be but might not be [
hellstart.whatistobebutmightnotbe.whatthehell.whenthen]
71] what is to be [hellstart.whatistobe.whatthehell.whenthen]
72] what can be but is never to be [
hellstart.whatcanbebutisnevertobe.whatthehell.whatthen]
73] what has been [hellstart.whathasbeen.whathehell.whenthen]
74] what is to be but now seems unlikely [
hellstart.whatistobebutnowseemsunlikely.whatthehell.whenthen]
75] what will be but is not [
hellstart.whatwillbebutisnot.whatthehell.whenthen]
76] what has been might still be [
hellstart.whathasbeenmightstillbe.whatthehell.whenthen]

77] what is to be but when [
hellstart.whatistobebutwhen.whatthehell.whenthen
78] what can be but ...only if...then [
hellstart.whatcanbebutonlyifthen.whatthehell.whenthen]
79] what can be but is not [
hellstart.whatcanbebutisnot.whatthehell.whenthen]
80] what is to be [hellstart.whatistobe.whatthehell.whenthen]
81] what is to be in time [
hellstart.whatistobeintime.whatthehell.whenthen]
82] what can be but...? [hellstart.whatcanbebut?.whatthehell.whenthen]
83] what is to be but if when and how [
hellstart.whatistobebutifwhenandhow.whatthehell.whenthen]
84] what will be [hellstart.whatwillbe.whatthehell.whenthen]
85] what was but can be still [
hellstart.whatwasbutcanbestill.whatthehell.whenthen]
86] what is to be but only if [
hellstart.whatistobebutonlyif.whatthehell.whenthen]
87] what is to be but only when [
hellstart.whatistobebutonlywhen.whatthehell.whenthen]
88] what if we can then what and how [
hellstart.whatifwecanthenwhatandhow.whatthehell.whenthen]
89] what has been and why [
hellstart.whathasbeenandwhy.whatthehell.whenthen]
90] what is to be [hellstart.whatistobe.whatthehell.whenthen]
91] what should be but [
hellstart.whatshouldbebut.whatthehell.whenthen]
92] what is to be [hellstart.whatistobe.whatthehell.whatthen]
93] what was but could be [
hellstart.whatwasbutcouldbe.whatthehell.whenthen]
94] what could be then but only if [
hellstart.whatcoukdbethenbutonlyif.whatthehell.whenthen]
95] what is to be [hellstart.whatistobe.whatthehell.whenthen]
96] what is to be but why [
hellstart.whatistobebutwhy.whatthehell.whenthen]
97] what if but could be [
hellstart.whatifbutcouldbe.whatthehell.whatthen]
98] if not now then when [
hellstart.ifnotnowthenwhen.whatthehell.whenthen
99] what could but is not [

hellstart.whatcouldbutisnot.whatthehell.whenthen]
100] if not this then what [
hellstart.ifnotthisthenwhat.whatthehell.whenthen]

WHAT HAPPENS TO THE SOUL ON DAY OF DEATH

Now that we have looked at the predefined parameters it's time to shock and awee you all first a ghost can rise as instantly as death occurs this is because of pre-installed and predefined parameters that talks to the soul [ghost] to guide it out of the body very fast as fast as a fraction of a second these are the brain commands

Now.exit.fast.entrypoint.you.exitpoint.human

Iftrappedwriggle.fast.ask.whereis.exit.fast

Ifnotdead.human.stopandaskcode4860.fast and when replied then proceed following reply.

1. You are not injured or facing death then stay in the body okay?

2. If death coming then ask for replacement of the spirit by acetate using;

Whenneardeathchooseforacetatetorepresentyouinheavenorhell.start

Whatistobecanbe.start

Followed by

Whatcanberevealednowfast.start

Instantly a message is replayed

David Gomadza first checking left and right God does not want you infact he said stay on earth represent wxyztstuvwxyz meaning humans with a little bit of godliness in them highlights

love for Yahweh and obedience to Yahweh and love for human race which are the strongest qualities of Yahweh
Now if we Ask another question then Yahweh is everywhere because of you never have Yahweh been so manifested in heaven and on earth than now all creatures sing Yahweh Yahweh
If we look at the clock of change Yahweh reckon humans might be the solution to future climatic changes which Yahweh himself admitted has no control over if we Ask what can be done then this is the answer Yahweh could also be represented in hell but only after defeating the devil through wisdom and shine darkness into light
Now if we look at Yahweh we can see that I have clearly identified who he is and can feel him even though I am human I can talk to Yahweh through the xyztuvwxyz meaning an aerial that has both ground radar as per translation and dimensions for GPS tracking system and this is how I have reconstructed everything ask why then the answer is that to prove Yahweh exist we must be able to connect to him and this is crucial .Ya is at frequency 789 Htz but his image is at frequency 764780386 meaning image is the radar while .Ya is [GPS tracking] the frequency at 789 but in reverse order meaning that if .Ya is the [GPS] frequency then his image is the radar.
Now let's compute how we can calculate these valued
If you ask what can be done to connect to Yahweh this is the answer humans have failed to master what is needed to connect to Yahweh until now that means only me [David Gomadza] is the only person who can connect to Yahweh.
Now if frequency is like his presence then .Ya is a value between 700 to 789 to be precise if we are to pin point .Yah on the map we can add a reference point in terms of time and place and this makes .Ya presence the same as my GPS tracker using our gadget we can find it as 78964321089284
Now Ask who are you and why you respond

I am the almighty Yahweh but disguised as xyztuvwxyz meaning Cherubum named Hezoborah this is because over years humans have tried to track me only to capture me and not to ask for help

Why is that so the answer I have powers to terminate everyone in a single episode of rage and pain what can be done then to those situation we can ask if we are all safe forever as humans the answer predefined parameters means humans forever will be safer only apart from 2084 when new electromagnetic waves enter the solar system

Now what is Yahweh to all Yahweh is the almighty king who resides above xyzttuvwxyzrsuvwxyz translation ocean land near Jerusalem above 08987645837890 north and 7890768928078 south but in disguise as the fierce Cherubum Hezoborah now if we Ask the coordinates what can they reveal coordinates reveal yourself and what you protect we can't instantly a flashing light nearly strikes me I ran but when I left Cherubum shown over me

A giant shadow with one big head and all in white tilting over me so I ask why you can use a lightning strike as before then it said [translation converting nerve impulses to action potentials]

I am the all mighty Yahweh if you dare see me say .amen

So I refused but somehow it removed the white suit to reveal nothing at all but a huge gusty wind with the following formula which I obtained ask why and not how this giant gusty wind just kept rolling like sea waves but without doing anything Yahweh would have roared but on inspection that was only a disguise Yahweh was the white huge one head giant

This is his formula 01876582867802398 X 786487623108970294 X silkpastyx100000000000 X 10 to power 9

Where 01876582867802398 is a material found only in heaven called acetate fibriolisis like acetate that cannot be killed by shaking

Code 786487623108970294 is acetate X acetate eletatete is an energy bases acetate that eats others for fuel
Now if we add a voice through acetate original and wireless transmitter then Yahweh is a hidden small transmitter inside that can be pulled out but without anything happening to it because everything else depends on it but can't be destroyed
Now if we look at the equations again this becomes clear that acetate is a disguised form of Yahweh on a small scale if we are to ask what can be then this is the answer If Yahweh could communicate with humans his goal in creation was to find a clever human who can decode all this and now that I have done this then we might as well start new creation because I can create anything just by looking at it I am the first live acetate even greater than Ya because Ya forever will only remain invisible whereas I can be both now Ask acetate to hide you the inner me can't but the outer can but in reverse if we Ask the real me now to hide then it's impossible because mass X matter makes live impossible for all this Now say David you hide then a different person hides this proves that we have 4 human beings in every one of us this is your task proof beyond doubt that now after writing a book about humans having 4 souls or brains here are all the souls
1 David the acetate who can't hide but ask you to hide instead this is the flesh me
2. Say hide anyone to avoid capture and listen carefully
David David what are you trying to do scaring all of us like you did in Bradford
Now Ask what can be done and listen David can ask me for advice instead of ..shocked the real me [David] but why you clone us if you have your original this defies logic
David 4 I sent you on a mission what did you find but I was to tell you and you said wait and then I have been waiting okay tell me Jesus man that's so wrong if I Ask why then what's your response a missionary must deliver the news on time not wait

okay I apologize now what is the future like
Amazed we rule the world from 2026 in March after the third world War that killed almost all the West after Russia dropped xyvxyzuvw meaning nuclear radiation on USA that melts everyone but Joe Biden
Now let's Ask why a world War is possible this is the answer all countries have exhausted their weaponry now but are hiding the fact from all of us because weapons stock piles are 70 percent down than last year all countries are hoping for a truce but Iran will ask everyone to use their weapons on the USA for a change because all weapons used in all global wars are manufactured in USA the world is going to agree but this trigger a world War that the West will initially win but this is to change the power shield that Russia will accelerate nuclear even though now they haven't started they will become the richest country on earth through xyzttuvw meaning trust and getting paid for protection money
Now if we Ask what can be done now I advise you pay us protection money instead of 87898260 per country from today the reason being that we are now officially the owners of Antarctica you will see because we claimed Antarctica and their rules are based on a working rules based order and if that fails Antarctica will become ours meaning the only safe inhabitants country on earth this will mean everyone asking as for help as everywhere else the land will be in habitable
To know this is the truth ask why the answer is that the USA has recently signed a pack with Britain to deploy nuclear weapons in case it is struck and can't act back fast on the attacker that means Moscow can be attacked as well just as Britain can be attacked by Belarus
Now the only stubborn country is Iran because of the suffering at the hands of the USA ,through sanctions
Now if we add Hezoborah to the equation we have God in disguise meaning the real Yahweh on Iranian side hence the

triggering of world War 3
Now what if that does not happen that way I have been to the future I have seen this war
Now back to the theme of the book if a spirit dies it goes into panic mode this is so because without panic the risks of being trapped in a dead body are high if in distress humans act slow because they have to think unlike acetate or spirit that follows clearly defined parameters if we Ask why then this is the answer
The spirit simply responds well a billion times better than humans to code than to thoughts
Here are the codes
1 exitfastandsafe.start
2 ifnotthenriskofbeingtrappedishigh.start
3 whatif.start
4 whatthen.start
5 whatcanbe.start
6 whatwillbe.start
7 whatistobe.start
8 whatcanbe.start
9 whatwillbe.start
10 whatcanbe.start
11 whatis.start
12 whatcanbe.start
13 whatwouldbe.start
14 whatis.start
15 whatwouldbe.start
16 whatwillbe.start
17 whatistobe.start
18 whatcanbebut.start
19 whatistobe.start
20 whatwastobe.start
21 whatistobe.start
22 whatcanbe.start
23 whatwillbe.start

24 whatwascanbe.start
25 whatistobe.start
26 whatistobebutwhy.start
27 whatistobebutcantbe.start
28 whendeadstart.runfastout.start
29 whenfrightenedactfastout.start
30 whatif.start
31 thengotoheaven
32 whenthenthengotohell.start
33 toheaventhenaskfor.Ya
34 tohellthenaskfor.devil
35 ifstuckinsidebodydelegatetoacetatefast.start
36 whatcanbesaidnow.start
37 askwhatthehell.whenthen
39 ask.why
40 askwhatcanbe.start
41 askwhatcouldbe.start
42 askwhen.start
43 askwhatis.start
44 ifindistressrun.start
45 runoutofthebodyto.Ya.start
46 walk to.devil.start
47 askfor.Ya
48 askfor.devil
49 askwhatis.start
50 whatcanbe.start
51 whatcanbedone.start
52 whatistobe.start
53 whatisandwas.start
54 whatwasandwhy.start
55 whatcanbe.start
56 whatistobe.start
57 whatcanbe.start
58 whatistobeistobebutwhen.start

59 ifindoubtthenstopbutstart.start
60 neverignorecallstoexit.start
61 exit.start
62 exit.fast.start
63 exit.fast.now
64 whatcanbe.start
65 whatifthenwhat.start
66 whatcanbebut.start
67 whatistobebutwhen.start
68 whatwouldbe.start
69 whatcanbebut.start
70 whatwillbe.start
71 whatisbutwhen.start
72 whatwillbebutstart.start
73 whatisthenwhatcanbe.start
74 whatistobe.now
75 whatisthenwhy.start
76 afterexitthenwhat.start
77 wheninheaven.ask.ya
78 wheninhell.ask.devil
79 whatifweask.start
80 whatcanbebuthow.start
81 whatcouldbebuthow.start
83 whatwasbuthowthenstart.start
84 whatcouldbebutwhy.start
85 whatistobethenwhy.start
86 whatistobe.start
87 whenindoubt.start
88 whatcanbebut.start
89 whatwillbe.start
90 whatis.start
91 whatistobe.start
92 whatwasbutisnot
93 whatwouldbebuthowcome.start

94 whenbuthow.start
95 whatifbuthow.start
96 whatistobe.start
97 whatcanbe.start
98 whatwouldbebutstart.now.start
99 toexithitthesepressurepointsinorder.start
100 askwhatif.start
101 whatistobe.start
102 whatcanbe.start
103 whatistobe.start
104 whatwillbe.start
105 whatcanbe.start
106 whathasbeensaid.when
107 whatwillbesaid.when
108 howcanweknow.start
109 whatifnowoutsidebody.start
110 whatwillbe.start
111 whatcanbe.start
112 whatistobe.start
113 whathasbeen.start
114 whatwillbe.start
115 whatistobe.start
116 whatcanbebutwhen.start
117 whatistobe.start
118 tobeistobe.start
119 whatcanbesaid.start
120 whatisnowifnotthenstart.start
121 whathasbeen.start
122 ifnotwhatthen.start
123 whatistobe.start
124 whatistobe.when
125 whatthenandwhy.start
126 whatcanbe.start
127 whatififoutside.then.start

128 what.is.start
129 whatistobe.start
130 whatwas.start
131 whatwouldbebutwhen.start
132 whatcouldbe.start
Now if we Ask the same questions from 133 to 150 now adding hellstart.question.whatthehell.whenthen
This is the answer
133 hellstart.whatcouldbe.whatthehell.whenthen
134 hellstart.whatwas.whatthehell.whenthen
135 hellstart.whatcanbesaidandwhy.whatthehell.whenthen
136 hellstart.whatiswhyandwhen.whatthehell.whenthen
137 hellstart.whatis.whatthehell.whenthen
138 helplstart.whatcanbe.whatthehell.whenthen
139 hellstart.whatistobe.whatthehell.whenthen
140 hellstart.whatistobe.whatthehell.whenthen
141 hellstart.whatcanbe.whatthehell.whenthen
142 hellstart.whatistobe.whatthehell.whenthen
143 hellstart.whatwasbutcouldbe.whatthehell.whenthen
144 hellstart.whatwastobe.whenthen
145 hellstart.whatcoulbeifthenwhat.whatthehell.whenthen
146 hellstart.whatistobe.whatthehell.whenthen
147 hellstart.whatisbutcannotbe.whatthehell.whenthen
148 hellstart.whatistobe.whatthehell.whenthen
149 hellstart.whatistobe.whatthehell.whenthen h
150 hellstart.whatcouldbe.whatthehell.whenthen
Now we have looked at the critical codes let us look further at who gives these instructions we can see that there is a prerecorded message in the system using acetate that automatically replays itself in case of death
Now Ask yourself any question regarding death death is the final chapter of human life as such must be feared those who fear death live longer
Now Ask what if you can't challenge death because those who

challenge death work up dead what can be done a lot of questions can be done that means that if we Ask what is then what is the reply what is is the fact that death has never been defeated it is God's plan that all man fall by death alone if man has to live forever then what is the purpose of life and creation? Now let's Ask a lot of questions like when spirit exit the body where does it go and why and how it know where to go the spirit on death go to heaven or death we now know the route is a predefined route guided by our actions that means we can control where we go we can control not to go to hell but chose heaven and vice verse

If I Ask what can be done this is the answer A soul can be trapped inside the body denying it an opportunity to present itself to .Ya or the .devil as per the creation agreement verse2 that reads in case you are not happy about the first amendment decision then you have the chance to choose to present your case before .Ya or .devil

10 verses of the Creation commandment

1. Live as you will by the creation agreement
2. Live for yourself and not for others
3 thou shall ask if not sure about how to live
4 what is to be is to be after death and can not be challenged after
5 when death comes you shall exit according to the way you chose to live
6 exit to hell or death as per path of your life
7 ask what if or what then for heaven or hell respectively
8 ask what can be done before you [spirit] exit the body
9 ask what could be just after exit
10 what if If you can challenge the creator what then if you can challenge the devil but overall the system is fair

Now that you know the rules of creation we can look at how spirits become ghosts the difference is that things have stopped whereas on the other hand it's like the continuation of life ghosts represents spirits in a different dimension this means that as we speak ghosts can't process and know what is being talked about whereas spirits can because the spirit is acetate whereas ghosts are electromagnetic waves

Now if we Ask a ghost why this is the reply just because I can exist like this means I must and this has nothing to do with the creator or the afterlife nor the devil whereas the spirit has everything to do with the creator and the devil if we Ask a spirit why this is the answer I am a spirit going to Yahweh for judgement asked if afraid of hell this is the answer hell is just like heaven in spirit form the difference is the road you took if you when you lived like a human being

Now what really does happen when a person dies this is the answer when a person dies something trigger the death socket if we Ask what then this is the answer The spirit groove activates as signs of death becomes evident a ball of spirit emotions rolls down the spirit groove so fast that it is like lightning in speed

Now this is exactly what happens to a soul when a person dies

1 soul spirit ball rolls down the spirit groove into the spirit socket

2 when this happens the spirit then activates the spirit receptor sockets These are sockets to activate for exit only when there is no death these will never light on

3 the spirit itself asks several questions in successive

a can I exit now

b how fast and where is life

c is dwarg this means that whatever happens ceteris paribus I will insist on a plan that I must carryout effectively and this means exiting safely to heaven or hell

Now let's trace exact path

4 once in the socket groove wriggle body Once and ask what if

5 ask whatthehell.whenthen

6 ask what was and what is now

7 ask what can be done

8 ask whereas
9 ask who then
10 ask what is to be is to be
11 wait for response and then ask what is to be
12 wait for a response and ask what can be
13 what would be
14 what might be
15 what could be
Exit socket and escape to the frontal lobby if the head [the victim is a gunshot victim shot in the temple head right side but for the purpose of this task - so that his soul goes to heaven to deliver a message to Allah same as .Ya]
Once in the right frontal lobby of the head it must enter the exit socket that is there but probably has never used as this is the only case study where the spirit exited the head because of the gunshot wound
Now if we Ask what is the normal way in such circumstances then the answer is that the spirit must exit through the right side of the head in normal circumstances these are the commands
1. Enter socket
2 activate it but wait for the voice [acetate warning voice of the risks of death of the soul if it doesn't escape
3 now it must push the following points
I the upper drawer of the brain which activates exit point
ii the lower drawer that activates until now the middle jaws of the mouth that release a socket like structures that locks the spirit inside it ready to eject it out to road to heaven or hell
iii the red only active sockets that teaches the spirit what to do in a fraction of a socket the teaching instructions if in distress that means death is coming not just to the body but to you as well
Now let's continue with point 4 above
4 when a body is to die the spirit must exit fast This is the route

I first jump in the air to get acetate eletatetete this is some form of energy burning fuel instead of accumulating energy that means now everything the spirit comes into contact with will become its fuel that it can grow from a peanut size you a large ball of fire like material

Now when this ball rolls into the receptor socket it kick starts some bouncing where it must hit a socket to activate that socket ready to act on it that means following this path

1. Enter right to live socket and activate it

2 right to choose socket to decide where to go even though we now know that is already predefined

3 the exit only socket the ball bounces off a socket that can trigger the escape of the other spirit still trapped inside [the real human soul that simply goes to Yahweh

Now if we are to ask then this is the answer .Ya expects all souls to go to him but overtime some have become clever enough to know that creation was meant to increase .Yah' s fuel consumption instead of going to look for fuel instead all fuel would come looking for him [not trying to put you off creation but read with an open eyes

Now let's continue the spirit must also hit the socket where in lands on a piglike structure inside the head on a person when this piglike structure is hit then something that talks like a talking pig comes out warning of the risks of death then soon after the pig itself then a new voice comes out of the pig saying don't waste time listening to the pig it's just good for breakfast instead listen to the voice of .Ya the voice then stops when another terrifying loud voice says .Ya I was so clever waiting for you now that you are here let's the braining begin I am the creator the I am but without the what am I this is because the what I am is you that means you completes me you and me is the I Am What I am

If we are to ask why this is so this is the reply this is because the sockets are arranged in such a way that if I am then you ask me

What I am that means you simply need to ask what I am to complete the sockets ask me what and find out for yourself What the answer I am with something goes down our belly to the index feet on the right foot if we trace there then this is the answer I am What I Am this is because I am if asked What converts to I am What I am but still this is confusing because it's God why would the almighty king want to associate himself with a dead spirit? The answer .Ya must make sure that each spirit must exist as well and for it to exist then it must be part of the large spirit world that is spearheaded by Yahweh but if we look closely this in reality causes the attachment of something xyzwtrstuvwsstuv meaning a fuel drip that can collet the fuel first then burn it even though the spirit don't know this if we Ask. Ya why he conceal this when it's obvious he replies humans have literally became a huge waste of time and opportunity that means we must aim higher to please .Ya
Now let's continue with the journey if we trace the path in the body something hits these points so fast and immediately exists the body fast
1. Central lobby of the brain [where the tree of life starts - it ends in the anus]
2 the altoabei which is just above the hippocampus that activates the speech of the voices that warns of death
3 the axlier that lies just above the angular herereid which is something that activates the piglike animal that literally talks
4 it hits also the heronoid abacus that hits the grand angular which in turn hits up the abcderer which activates .Ya inside all of us human beings but if you speak this word several times something keeps saying don't wake me up ...Yahweh and fades away
5 it hits up the angular acetate agererer that eventually starts to talk asking what can be done and when
6 once that has said that something else comes out at the same place but in mirror image and say ask.why but stops

7 this is followed by something else that asks what can be done
8 that is followed by something else that asks whenthen
9 that asks something to come out and presents its case
10 what can be this thing asks earnestly in a low voice just before the spirit exists looking at all this you can see that humans now don't only have the 4 brains of Yahweh they have the othersides representatives also which are the devils as it turns out altogether we have 8 different creatures that asks questions in that order

1 What can be - .Ya
2 What was - Catitighit
3 What is - Anna
4 What could be -Joseph

The bad side [hell-devil]

5 What could be - .devil
6 What is to be - Heries [wife]
7 What was to be - Amargeddeon
8 What should be - Herechercht [devil's best friend's wife]

[The devil is a mirror image of God]

Now let's Ask a lot of short questions
What see who answers 1
When 4
What then 5
Who 1
Was 2
If 1
Has 4
Then devils best friend 7
What could be 5
What would be 7
What is to be 3
What can be 1
Who was 3

What was 3
What could be 5
If I 1
If you 4
If we 4
Why not 4
What was but is not [Joseph and Anna] 3 & 4
What would be 5 & 7
What was before 2,3 & 4
What would be 6,7 & 8
What if but both sides good and bad mainly 1 & 5
If not now when 3
If us why not now 3 & 4 then 1 & 2
What could be but is not 3 & 4 and devil side 7 & 8
If not now when then devil side
What could be that is not but can be 3 & 4 and 7 & 8
What was but might not be 3 & 4 and 7 & 8 then 7 & 8
If we then why wait God's 4 heads
If not us when then devils side 4 heads
What can be that is to be but might not be 3 & 4 and 7 & 8 and 7 & 8

To conclude we can see why no human being would have ever mastered this it takes a smart brain the guts to leads and some serious thinking to decode God and creation and here at last the masterpiece.

You can never hear about all this anywhere else for whoever says so is lying DNA sequence

HasanyoneeverdecodedGodandhis4headsuntil.now.searchallbrainsknowntoman.start

Results just davidgomadza.start.universityofzimbabwe.ny.uk.ask

If we look at all this what does this mean to us as humans?

It means we are the slowest thinking animals on the planet for it took us billion of years to search and search in the right places and to ask and to ask the right questions

We did it as Tomorrow's World Order and as I [David Gomadza] congratulations humans.
To end here is the epic end to our spirit that went to God
On arrival it realized that it had died as fear sets in and instantly a huge thing just flew from nowhere and landed in front of it
Instantly it uncovers itself and asked why it was there so early than Yaweh had given it time
It looked confused at first then thought for a while it traces back to its last actions where deliberately walked to a flag planted showing a Lebanese flag but without knowing that these were grenades under it it kicked the flag and instantly a grenade detonated but it was actually a bomb triggered by someone watching possibly in a car that's when I intercepted the soul as it blew up and went with it to heaven [I am who I am above instantly attach for fuel]
But this took me to heaven
Where in confusion I was also the being in front of me but nevertheless this is what happened Catitighit asked me [my wife] what do we do with souls that come way too early isn't it hard to judge them?
Yes replied [me] but we can't accept these anywhere what xyzttuvwzyztt can they have for us?
Translation means reach vocabulary of acetate we can use to build our reserves that can point also to the fact that over the years Yahweh collects vocabulary based on time of the people he has to judge
Now let's see what happened to our poor soul Yahweh through some commands First bundled up the message sent by this soul message
Israel is killing souls for money without the money given out in fact its fatar
If fatar is for you Allah for your fuel still its wrong because these souls are xxttrrstuvwxyz meaning not ready for commercial use that alone triggers fatijahid and we shall deliver

without delay a jihadini that will make all obey us until kingdom come
Instantly a ball rolls out of the soul into the air consuming the words somehow displaying in air and the ball flips to the intwinned couple who the woman Anna instantly digested and sent nerve impulses and Action Potentials to Yahweh ' s best friend who reads the message but inhales it in his lungs where it dissolves into air they all breath and instantly all knew what the message about.
Instantly Yahweh said "acetate ete ete eta eta eta eta eta " and instantly all souks that committed suicide are stuck on something rolling before instantly melting to boiling point and Yahweh raised his right hand and sucked all and instantly something inside his hand closed at the other end where they went and instantly he squeezed his hand until all liquid is absorbed
Once absorbed something like vocabulary codes are sucked into the system and all started hearing all these new words.
The end

ABOUT THE AUTHOR

Visit www.twofuture.world

www.ingramcontent.com/pod-product-compliance
Lightning Source LLC
Chambersburg PA
CBHW051403250726
48656CB00006B/2240

* 9 7 9 8 3 2 3 6 9 4 0 5 1 *